SUPER PARKS!

GRAND CANYON NATIONAL PARK

by James Buckley Jr.

arcadia®
CHILDREN'S BOOKS

Published by Arcadia Children's Books
A Division of Arcadia Publishing
Charleston, SC
www.arcadiapublishing.com

Super Cities is a trademark of Arcadia Publishing, Inc.

First published 2022

Manufactured in the United States.

ISBN 978-1-4671-9891-2

Library of Congress Control Number: 2022937947

Notice: The information in this book is true and complete to the best of our knowledge. It is offered without guarantee on the part of the author or Arcadia Publishing. The author and Arcadia Publishing disclaim all liability in connection with the use of this book.

Produced by Shoreline Publishing Group LLC
Santa Barbara, California
Designer: Patty Kelley

Contents

WELCOME TO THE
Grand Canyon!

What's the big deal about a big hole in the ground? Well, when the hole is so big it is considered one of the United States's most awe-inspiring attractions, it becomes a pretty big deal! Grand Canyon National Park is centered on the deep, narrow area in Arizona that gives the park its name. The Grand Canyon was formed over millions of years by the Colorado River. More than a mile deep, the Grand Canyon has thrilled and amazed countless visitors over the years. It not only boasts stunning views,

but it also has miles of hiking trails, new bike trails on each rim, and hundreds of animal species. There really is nowhere else like it on Earth.

To see the Grand Canyon, you have to go to the National Park that surrounds it. Inside this book, you'll find more about the canyon's history, the people who once lived there, the things you can do and see, and how to enjoy your visit. So get ready for one GRAND adventure!

GRAND CANYON: Map It!

Grand Canyon National Park is located in the north-central part of the state of Arizona. The canyon and the park run mostly east to west, following the path of the Colorado River, which still flows through the bottom of the canyon. The main visitor areas are on the South Rim and the North Rim. The South Rim is about 75 miles north of Flagstaff, Arizona. The North Rim is reached by driving south from near the small town of Bitter Springs, Arizona, which is near the state's border with Utah. The Kaibab National Forest is adjacent to most of the park, while the Navajo Nation and the Hopi Reservation are to the east.

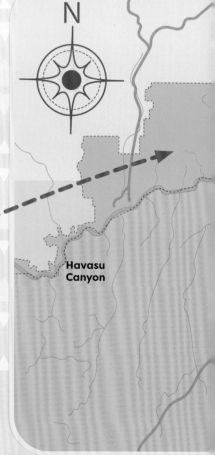

N

Havasu Canyon

ARIZONA

Grand Canyon National Park

MEXICO

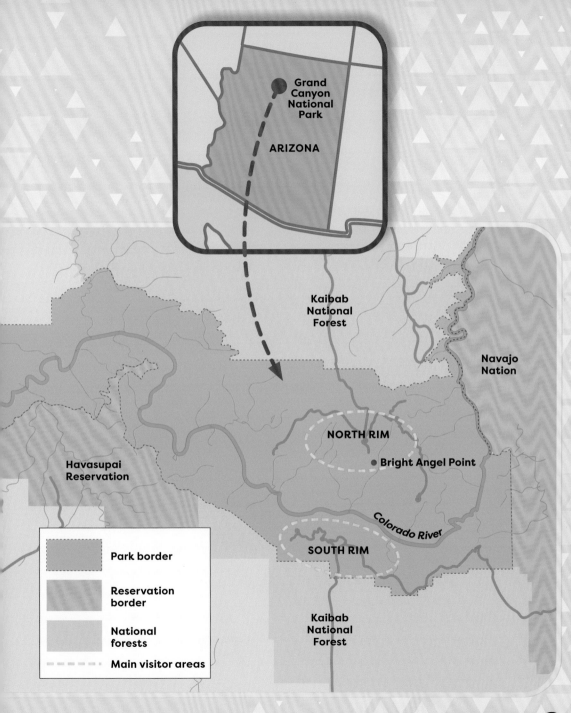

Grand
Canyon
National
Park

ARIZONA

Kaibab
National
Forest

Navajo
Nation

NORTH RIM

● Bright Angel Point

Havasupai
Reservation

Colorado River

SOUTH RIM

	Park border
	Reservation border
	National forests
- - -	Main visitor areas

Kaibab
National
Forest

NORTH RIM

Visitors to the Grand Canyon can only start their trip from one of two places: the North Rim and the South Rim. The North Rim is, not surprisingly, on the north side of the canyon. Of the two rims, it is the least visited. There are fewer places to stay and it's a bit harder to get to; there's a long drive through a forest landscape on a twisty road. Of course, fewer visitors means smaller crowds! Also, the North Rim is more than 1.5 miles in elevation (which is the distance of land above sea level). It gets cold and snowy in winter and is mostly closed then. But summer visitors can choose from dozens of hiking trails.

Bright Angel Point
With a sweeping view toward the distant South Rim, this is one of the most popular spots on the North Rim. Plan your family photos here with the canyon in the background!

Grand Canyon Lodge

This is the biggest place to stay on the North Rim. Built originally in 1928, it was later rebuilt in 1936. It's the only place to stay indoors on the North Rim, so you have to plan ahead and make reservations. There are also some places to camp.

Skiers Only

Expert cross-country skiers are allowed into the North Rim part of the park during snowy winters. It's not for everyone, but if you love winter sports, this is for you!

SOUTH RIM

This is what people usually picture when they think of the Grand Canyon. Because this part of the park is closer to a major freeway, and because it has more places for people to stay and eat, the crowds are much bigger. Try coming in spring or fall when crowds are a bit smaller. Whenever you make it, however, you'll be treated to breathtaking views and tons of things to do and see. Remember, the South Rim is still more than a mile in elevation; you might need a little while to get used to the thin air!

Grand Canyon Village
This is the main visitor area on the South Rim. You'll find shops, restaurants, places to stay, and lots of maps and information.

Drive or Not Drive?

The South Rim can get pretty crowded in the summer. Your family can leave the car in the town of Tusayan and take a shuttle to Grand Canyon Village. There are also shuttles that go between key sites on the South Rim.

Hermit Road

Summer means shuttles only on this scenic drive. They wind along the South Rim, to the west of the Village, stopping at the best viewpoints. You can also ride rental bikes here or hike.

Desert View Drive

Your car is allowed on this route, which goes east from the Village, connecting more than a dozen jaw-dropping places to see the canyon.

HAVASU CANYON

Most of the areas around the Grand Canyon National Park are great places for families and kids of all ages. But Havasu Canyon should be on the "things to do when older" list. It is about 35 miles west of Grand Canyon Village, outside the park boundaries. But it is very hard to reach. Visitors have to drive on bouncy dirt roads and then make a long hike into the canyon. They'll reach Supai Village, home of the Havasupai. Though forcibly removed in the 1800s, the Havasupai people got their land back from Arizona in 1975. Today, they control the canyon and limit the number of visitors to help keep this beautiful place safe.

FAST FACT
About 400 people live in Supai year-round. They have their mail delivered by a mule rider!

With reservations, you can camp or stay at a small lodge near Supai. Pack mules can also be hired to carry gear.

Havasu Falls

The most famous attraction in Havasu Canyon is Havasu Falls and the spectacular blue-green water. Floods over the centuries have carved out the path of the falls. Minerals in the water, which is safe to swim in, create magical colors.

CANYON GEOLOGY

Have you ever watched flowing water carve a path through sand or dirt? Now multiply that by a gazillion. That's what happened to form the Grand Canyon. The Colorado River took more than six million years to scour out the enormous hole that we call the Grand Canyon. It's still carving today, about six inches every thousand years (which is pretty slow by human standards, so don't just sit there watching it!). That rate is much slower than when the river was really powerful, so don't expect the canyon to change much any time soon.

Layer Cake
Geologists count 11 layers of rock from the top to the bottom of the canyon. They include layers of sandstone, limestone, shale, and schist. The Kaibab Limestone layer at the top (you're standing on it!) was exposed about 270 million years ago.

More Than a River

Rain has also played a part in eroding the canyon. The North Rim has been most affected. Rain flows into the canyon from that rim, carrying stone and dirt with it.

Now THAT's Old!

The oldest rocks in the canyon are found, not surprisingly, at the bottom. They are called gneiss (pronounced "NICE") and were formed 1.8 billion years ago!

A History Mystery

The layers of the Grand Canyon can be dated accurately by geologists. However, there is a strange gap in the ages of the layers near the bottom. The oldest type of rocks are 1.8 billion years. But then the layer above it dates more than 500 million years more recently. Between other layers, the difference in age is much less; most are less than 100 million years. The big difference between those bottom layers baffles scientists; they expect the ages to be closer together. They call the narrow layer the Great Unconformity—that means it doesn't have the same age differences as other places!

RUSHING RIVER!

Down, down, down below the rims of the canyon, you can see a thin blue ribbon. That's the Colorado River, which flows from east to west through the Grand Canyon. The river starts in the Rocky Mountains in Colorado. It flows southwest through Utah before entering Arizona. After pouring through Lake Powell (see box), it carves along the Grand Canyon. To the west, it empties into Lake Mead before heading south. It forms the western edges of Nevada before reaching the Gulf of California. From start to end, the river is more than 1,450 miles (2.3 km) long.

The Battle for Dams

Mighty flowing rivers can generate power for electricity. The flowing water turns huge turbines that generate electricity. In 1963, after a long battle with conservationists, the Glen Canyon Dam (below) was built on the Colorado River northeast of the canyon. The dam created the enormous Lake Powell. The water that flowed through the dam created a huge amount of electricity. In 1933, the Hoover Dam was built to the west of the canyon to make Lake Mead. In between, the rushing river continues to flow through the Grand Canyon.

Darn Dams

Dams are huge cement barriers built to stop or control flowing water. The river water still flows through the dam, but it flows through machines. The water turns the machines, called turbines, which create electricity for homes and businesses. So that's good. But the flow of the river is, of course, changed. So that also changes how the river carves the rock downstream, and how animal life can move and live in the lower levels of water. The world needs electricity, but the world needs rivers, too. Putting up a dam is often a debate between those two needs.

Tens of millions of years ago, the area where the Grand Canyon formed was flat as a pancake. Atop the massive Colorado Plateau, the land was mostly desert and stone. But the Colorado River began doing its work. About 30-50 million years ago, the flow of water began to erode (wear away over time) the land, *sloooowly* forming a canyon that grew and grew over millions of years. Eventually, the river's scouring power created what we see today.

Layer Up: The Earth is made up of layers of rock, each laid down over tens of millions of years. Some layers were formed after glaciers moved through. Others were deposited by volcanic activity. Still others were made up of dirt left behind when enormous bodies of water evaporated. The Colorado River slowly cut through all those layers. They can be seen clearly on the walls of the canyon. Cool science word: This is called "stratification."

Setting the Table: The Colorado Plateau is a large geological area, centered around the place where four US states meet: Arizona, Colorado, Utah, and New Mexico. About 60 million years ago, huge and powerful underground forces started forming this vast, flat area. It became the cake that the river carved into.

UT

CO

Colorado Plateau

Wupatki/Sunset Crater Volcano

NM

AZ

Camels in the Canyon: The Ice Age happened about 20,000 years ago. Huge sheets of ice stretched down from the Arctic to cover most of North America. The wet conditions as the ice melted over thousands of years helped unusual animals thrive in the canyon. The place where visitors roam today was once home to mammoths, large camels, and the enormous Shasta ground sloth. They left behind footprints (above) and fossilized poop (right).

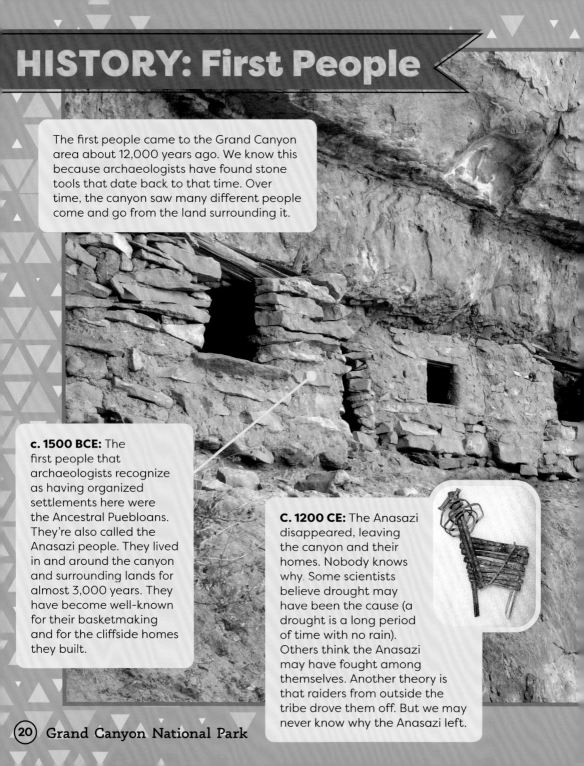

HISTORY: First People

The first people came to the Grand Canyon area about 12,000 years ago. We know this because archaeologists have found stone tools that date back to that time. Over time, the canyon saw many different people come and go from the land surrounding it.

c. 1500 BCE: The first people that archaeologists recognize as having organized settlements here were the Ancestral Puebloans. They're also called the Anasazi people. They lived in and around the canyon and surrounding lands for almost 3,000 years. They have become well-known for their basketmaking and for the cliffside homes they built.

C. 1200 CE: The Anasazi disappeared, leaving the canyon and their homes. Nobody knows why. Some scientists believe drought may have been the cause (a drought is a long period of time with no rain). Others think the Anasazi may have fought among themselves. Another theory is that raiders from outside the tribe drove them off. But we may never know why the Anasazi left.

New Arrivals: Not long after the Anasazi left, the Hopi people arrived. They came to revere the canyon as a special and spiritual place. About six hundred years ago, the Navajo people moved into the area of the North Rim. The Havasupai and Halupai also eventually made homes in land near the Grand Canyon.

Spanish Influence: Beginning in the early 1500s, Spanish soldiers looking for gold arrived in North America. The first people from Europe who saw the Grand Canyon arrived there in 1540. Unlike in other areas of Mexico and the Americas, the Spanish soldiers did not attack the local people. They left them alone. They also brought the first horses and sheep to the Southwest. Both animals became important parts of life for the people who lived there.

Grand Canyon National Park 21

HISTORY: Explorers Arrive

In 1848, the United States won a war against Mexico. The US took over land controlled by Mexico in the Southwest, including the Grand Canyon. The area had been visited briefly by Americans before, including a trip by a fur trapper named Ewing Young in 1826. Young traveled widely in the West, including many trips to California. But the canyon was so huge and so hard to explore, very little was known about it. That was about to change.

Here Comes Powell: The US government wanted to explore the Grand Canyon in a big way. However, the trip down the rapidly flowing Colorado River would be very dangerous. John Wesley Powell, a former Union Army soldier with only one arm, volunteered to lead the expedition. Many doubted that he would come back alive.

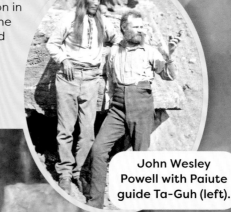

John Wesley Powell with Paiute guide Ta-Guh (left).

Starting Out: Powell set out from Green City, Wyoming, with four boats and 11 men. The first part of their trip was pretty smooth, much like the river in that part of the western canyon. However, about two weeks into the trip, they hit the first rapids. They were using wooden boats, so the men had a very hard time dealing with the super-fast water and the dangerous rocks alongside and in the river.

JOHN WESLEY POWELL

1869 EXPEDITION

6¢ U.S. POSTAGE

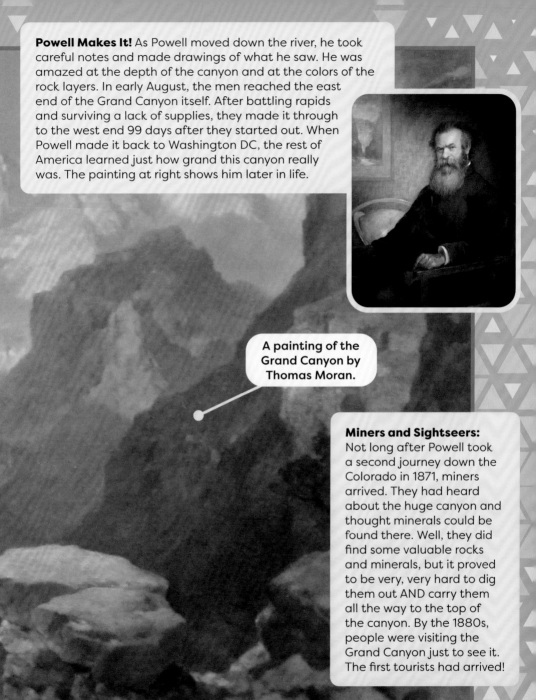

Powell Makes It! As Powell moved down the river, he took careful notes and made drawings of what he saw. He was amazed at the depth of the canyon and at the colors of the rock layers. In early August, the men reached the east end of the Grand Canyon itself. After battling rapids and surviving a lack of supplies, they made it through to the west end 99 days after they started out. When Powell made it back to Washington DC, the rest of America learned just how grand this canyon really was. The painting at right shows him later in life.

A painting of the Grand Canyon by Thomas Moran.

Miners and Sightseers: Not long after Powell took a second journey down the Colorado in 1871, miners arrived. They had heard about the huge canyon and thought minerals could be found there. Well, they did find some valuable rocks and minerals, but it proved to be very, very hard to dig them out AND carry them all the way to the top of the canyon. By the 1880s, people were visiting the Grand Canyon just to see it. The first tourists had arrived!

In 1901, the first railroad reached the South Rim of the canyon. This made it easier than ever for visitors to marvel at the incredible sight. But it soon became clear that all this activity needed to be organized or the canyon could be overrun or damaged.

A mule ride trip into the canyon in 1909!

SEP. 29. 09.
NO. 96.

1908: President Theodore Roosevelt made the entire Grand Canyon a wildlife refuge. He wanted to preserve the animals and plants of the area from the growing number of tourists. He wanted to do more despite objections from some miners (since they would no longer be able to work in the canyon), but Congress couldn't agree on how to protect the area.

1912: Arizona became a state. This opened up new ways to protect the canyon, which was now officially part of a US state.

1919: President Woodrow Wilson signed a law forming the Grand Canyon National Park. The Park grew over time to include the Kaibab Forest areas.

Grand Canyon Pioneers

Grand Canyon National Park wouldn't be what it is today without some truly amazing people who helped shape the park. Here are a few who made a difference during the area's early years.

Clarence Dutton, Geologist, 1841–1912

A former Civil War officer, Dutton joined Powell's later trips to learn about how the Grand Canyon was formed. Dutton's observations and measurements showed for the first time the many layers of the canyon itself. He led the way for other geologists to study the Grand Canyon (and other places) that revealed the age and history of the Earth.

Mary Colter, Architect, 1869–1958

Starting with the Hopi House next to the El Tovar Hotel, Colter designed some of the park's most beautiful and famous buildings. Unlike other architects of her time, she looked to native art for inspiration. Among her designs was Phantom Ranch, Bright Angel Lodge, and Desert View Watchtower. Look for images of all three elsewhere in our book.

Miner Tillotson
Superintendent, 1886–1955

Tillotson was in charge of the Grand Canyon for the National Park Service from 1927 to 1938. Using money from the national Works Project Administration, he led an important period of building. New trails were cut and managed, buildings added to both rims, and the staff was expanded. He also banned the killing of predatory animals in the park; this helped keep the balance of nature on track.

Ellsworth and Emory Kolb
Photographers
1876–1960; 1881–1976

Photography was still pretty new when people started coming to the Grand Canyon to sightsee. The Kolb brothers set up a photo studio near the South Rim in 1906. Their images were soon seen around the world, spreading the news about the canyon and attracting more and more visitors. Their rim-side photo studio can still be visited in its original location.

GRAND CANYON TODAY

The Grand Canyon itself has not changed a lot since those first people arrived 12,000 years ago. But in the last century, there have been a lot more people arriving. The national park now receives more than six million visitors a year. It's one of the most popular national parks; for most activities, reservations are needed. So tell your folks to plan ahead!

In the Winter, Go South
Nearly all of the North Rim's facilities are closed in the winter, when the area is usually very cold and often snowy. That part of the park usually closes by mid-October. The South Rim, though, is open year-round.

Avoiding Crowds
Summer is by far the busiest time of the year at the Grand Canyon, especially on the South Rim. If you can go in spring or fall, you'll see the same amazing views, but with fewer people around. If you have to go in summer, plan ahead and expect to wait in lines for parking, food, and some activities.

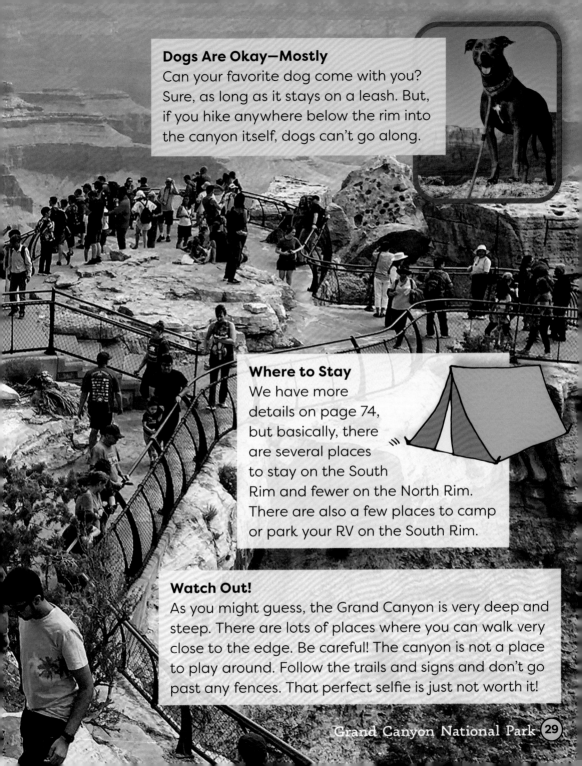

Dogs Are Okay—Mostly

Can your favorite dog come with you? Sure, as long as it stays on a leash. But, if you hike anywhere below the rim into the canyon itself, dogs can't go along.

Where to Stay

We have more details on page 74, but basically, there are several places to stay on the South Rim and fewer on the North Rim. There are also a few places to camp or park your RV on the South Rim.

Watch Out!

As you might guess, the Grand Canyon is very deep and steep. There are lots of places where you can walk very close to the edge. Be careful! The canyon is not a place to play around. Follow the trails and signs and don't go past any fences. That perfect selfie is just not worth it!

Native Americans and the Park

As the history of the Grand Canyon shows, indigenous peoples have long lived in and around it. The land they controlled for hundreds of years, however, was mostly taken away from them by the United States starting in the mid-1800s. Relations between tribal nations and the government have been difficult, and often violent, throughout history. Things are better now, if not perfect. Here's a look at the tribal nations and tribes that continue to play a part in the life of this natural wonder.

Navajo: This is the largest indigenous nation in the United States, stretching over parts of three states at the eastern end of the Grand Canyon. The Navajo never lived in the canyon, but around it, and of course the Colorado River played a part in their lives for centuries. Find out more about Navajo culture at museums in Tuba City and Window Rock, Arizona.

Southern Paiute: These people live east of the northern Grand Canyon. They lived for hundreds of years in the forests there. They continue a long tradition of basket making.

Hopi: Completely surrounded by the Navajo Nation, the Hopi reservation is also east of the Grand Canyon. The Hopi are related to the original Puebloans who lived in the area thousands of years ago. The Hopi people believe all animals and plants come from the Colorado River and the canyon. Their small community is mostly farmers. The Hopi House (page 37) in Grand Canyon Village was modeled after their traditional architecture.

Havasupai: Their reservation is to the west of the main Grand Canyon Village along the South Rim. Very hardy adventurers can take four-wheel-drive cars or trucks to see the Havasupai village (right) as well as amazing waterfalls.

Hualapai: Go about 100 miles west from Grand Canyon Village and you'll find the home of the Hualapai. About 2,000 people from this tribal nation live here, mostly in the town of Peach Springs. They also operate the amazing SkyWalk attraction. Check it out on page 39.

Grand Canyon Weather

The huge difference in elevation at the canyon means that weather can be extreme. Some of the coldest temperatures in Arizona are found at the North Rim in winter. Some of the hottest are found down in the bottom of the canyon, such as at Phantom Ranch. The four seasons are pretty clear-cut throughout the park.

FAST FACT
Temperatures can climb 5.5 degrees for every 1,000 feet you climb down—and vice versa!

Summer
The hottest time of the year, naturally. Temperatures can be in the 80s at the rims, and more than 100 at the canyon bottom. Make sure to have **lots** of water handy if you visit in summer, and lots of sunscreen. Thunderstorms can happen often, too, including some with spectacular lightning.

Spring
Spring brings nicer weather after a hard winter, with more rain and wind. But because the rims of the canyon are at seven to eight thousand feet, spring can also still include periods of chillier weather and even some late-season snow.

Fall

This season is usually drier, but still warm, especially on the South Rim. However, the nights are much colder than they are in summer. A bonus for visitors in the fall is an amazing display of colors on the trees in many parts of the Kaibab National Forest, which surrounds the eastern end of the Grand Canyon.

Winter

As noted, the North Rim is so tough in winter that it is closed to nearly all visitors. The South Rim stays open, but it also gets a lot of snow and ice. Visitors should plan for driving in snow and should bring along lots of warm clothing. Long hikes are hard to make in winter, too. Views of the canyon can still be awesome, but snow, rain, or clouds can sometimes block the view.

Mather Point Near the Visitor Center, follow the crowds to this very popular viewpoint. You can see all the way to the North Rim, but you can't see to each end of the canyon. It's so huge that there is not one point from which you can see the whole thing!

Things to see in the Grand Canyon

On both canyon rims, dozens of spots are set up for amazing views. But there is more to do at the Grand Canyon than just stand there and say, "WOW!" We'll start on the South Rim.

Visitor Center

Start here to get all the info you need for your exploration of the canyon. There's a store, an info booth, maps, and shuttle stops to several parts of the South Rim.

Lookout Studio and Kolb Studio

Both of these older buildings are located right on the edge of the South Rim, offering amazing views. They also are part of canyon history. Lookout Studio was built in 1914 to create a large viewing platform. Kolb Studio (right) was home to the photography brothers who arrived there in 1906 (page 26).

More Places to See

Trail of Time How can you walk through millions of years in just a few minutes? Take a stroll on this exhibit near the Visitor Center. It's a visual timeline of Grand Canyon history. Each meter you walk equals one million years of history. The big story is the geology of the canyon; as you walk the trail, you see how each layer of the canyon was formed, and also how the Colorado River slowly carved out the canyon.

Yavapai Point From above, this looks like a big bump sticking out from the South Rim. At the end of the bump, you're farther "into" the canyon than almost anywhere on the South Rim. The views are spectacular in front, but also to each side, as you peer down into smaller canyons that stretch back behind you to the South Rim. Get your camera ready!

Hopi House The traditions of the Hopi and other native people of the Grand Canyon are celebrated here. The building is modeled after Hopi buildings, made with local stone and thatched roofing materials. Hopi people lived in the building for many years, demonstrating traditional crafts to visitors. Today, it's a store selling those crafts and others from the region.

Verkamp's Visitor Center John Verkamp and his descendants operated this center for more than 100 years, until passing it on to the National Park Service in 2008. It was a gift shop then, but is now another place for visitors to find info; look for it near the end of the Trail of Time.

More Places to See

Tusayan Ruins To imagine what life was like for ancient people, visit this South Rim site. It's home to the 800-year-old remains of Tusayan Pueblo buildings. Tours take you through houses, storerooms, and ceremonial chambers preserved for study.

Desert View Watchtower To the east of Grand Canyon Village is Desert View. There, visitors will find this incredible 70-foot-tall stone tower. While the views from the windows are great, it's actually the re-creations of native art inside that make this place so interesting. Hopi artist Fred Kabotie created murals, designs, and paintings that show traditional Hopi figures and symbols. See page 40 for more!

Grand Canyon SkyWalk Scared of heights? Turn the page—quick! This is one of the newest attractions at the Grand Canyon. It opened in 2007 on the Hualapai reservation, about 100 miles west of Grand Canyon Village. It's really in the national park, but it is on the South Rim—or should we say OVER the South Rim. The U-shaped structure juts out over a 3,600-foot (1079-m) drop straight down to the Colorado River.

Inside the Tower

The large circular painting tells the **Snake Legend of the Hopi**. Panel by panel, it shows the stages of the first person to go down the Colorado River.

In 1932, Hopi artist Fred Kabotie created murals and artwork on the walls of the Desert View Watchtower. The figures are from Hopi legends and traditions. Each floor of the five-story tower includes paintings, symbols, and figures. On the upper floors, artists Chester Dennis and Fred Geary re-created petroglyphs found elsewhere in the canyon.

Fred Kabotie

The sun

Visitors can look up from the bottom of the tower to the high ceiling, also painted by Kabotie.

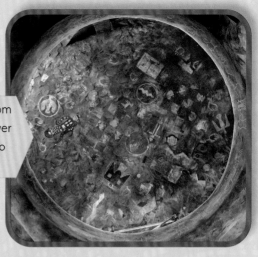

Muyingwa, a god of farming, holding a cornstalk.

Hayapao, a god of the air, with a rainbow above him

Preservation

Over the years, art experts have worked with Hopi artists to preserve the work of the artists. The tower is hit with rainstorms, dust clouds, snow, and ice. The paint can suffer in the elements, so work continues to preserve the colors and the beauty for the future.

North Rim Sights

Less crowded but just as beautiful, the North Rim doesn't have as much to do as the South Rim. But there is just as much to see!

Bright Angel Point This is the most popular viewing spot on the North Rim. It's a short walk from the Grand Canyon Lodge—but it's steep, so take your time. Remember, the North Rim is about 8,000 feet above sea level. So you'll feel the thin air! Use your eyes for the scenery, but use your ears, too. Listen for the Roaring Springs waterfall, which spurts out near the bottom of the canyon below you—more than 3,000 feet!

Grand Canyon Lodge Whether you stay here or just visit, it's worth a look. It was rebuilt in 1936 after a fire destroyed most of the original lodge. Check out the massive logs that make up the roof timbers, and the awesome views from several huge windows. If you want some luck, rub the shiny nose of the statue of Brighty the Mule, a character created in a children's book in the 1950s.

Point Imperial Up, up, and up: This is the highest viewing point in the entire national park. It has a great view to the east, making it perfect for sunrises (if you're a morning person!). From there you can see the Painted Desert in the distance, along with land belonging to the Navajo Nation, to the east of the National Park lands.

Walhalla Glades Step into this spot near the Walhalla Overlook and step back in time. Here you'll find remains of the ancient home of some Ancestral Puebloans. Parts of several walls are still standing, showing where rooms from a house or storage building were built more than 1,200 years ago.

Museums of the Canyon

Yavapai Geology Museum What do you call a museum as big as the Grand Canyon? That's sort of what this site is like. Along with displays about canyon geology and history, the Yavapai has a long, wide picture window. Below the window are maps, guides, and charts showing you just what you are looking at as you gaze at the colored, striped walls of the canyon in front of you. This museum is on the South Rim.

Bright Angel History Room Where can you see the whole canyon in one room? Right here! The incredible fireplace, designed by architect Mary Colter, includes rocks from every level of the Grand Canyon. They are layered to mirror the colors and ages of the canyon itself. Also on view are artifacts from the history of the Bright Angel Lodge and the national park.

Tuyasan Ruins and Museum

Remember these ruins from page 38? There's a museum to go along with them! You won't just see the 1,200-year-old ruins, you'll be able to learn more about them and the people who lived there. Plus, they have artifacts from even more ancient people, dating back thousands of years!

Experts Only!

The "biggest" museum in the Grand Canyon is not open to the public. Instead, the huge **Grand Canyon Museum Collection** is available to scientists, historians, and other people doing research. Items from the collection are put on display at different places around the canyon throughout the year, or travel to other museums. They've got ancient and recent baskets as well as John Wesley Powell's pocket watch.

It's a Train!

The first trains to the Grand Canyon left Williams, Arizona, in 1901. A steam train pulled the first cars. The trains stopped in 1969 as people chose to make the drive instead. However, in 1990, the old trains were restored and train service came back! The trip takes a bit over two hours and travels through beautiful desert and higher-elevation forests. The Grand Canyon Railway is now on the National Register of Historic Places.

Old and New Some trips still use the steam engines of old, but now they are powered by waste vegetable oil. Railroad fans love the old-time feel of the steam engines, which have been running on the Grand Canyon route since 1910!

Ride and a Show The train experience includes a Wild West shootout at the depot in Williams, and singing cowboys on the train. During the ride, watch out for cowboys riding alongside the rail cars—are they bandits or good guys?

Day Trip Some people stay at a fancy hotel in Williams and take the train to and from the canyon in a day. The train returns each evening from the canyon depot back to Williams.

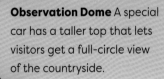

Observation Dome A special car has a taller top that lets visitors get a full-circle view of the countryside.

Hiking in the Canyon

There's no way you can see all of the Grand Canyon just by hiking. However, there is also no better way to get up close with the different parts of the canyon. People have been walking around and into the canyon for thousands of years—why not you? There are three ways to go:

Across the Rims This is the most popular way that visitors get out hiking. Trails along parts of both the South and North Rims, and through the forests in some places, offer ever-changing views of the canyon. They also give visitors a look at life and nature on the rims, from plants and trees to wildlife (great bird-watching!). Trails on the South usually start near the Visitor Center. On the North, trails start at the Lodge and other places. There also guided hikes with experts to show you more about what you're seeing.

Overnight and Backcountry Hikes If you and your family hike and camp, this might be a fun thing to try. But it's a challenge! You'll spend two or three days making a long hike into the canyon. You'll spend a night or two either on the bottom of the canyon or in one of the many backcountry spots on either rim. Wait until you see the stars at night over your campsite! Incredible! These hikes take a lot of planning, sometimes more than a year ahead.

Into the Canyon The most important thing to remember is that what goes down (you!) must come back up. Trails that head into the canyon can be steep and twisty. Going down will seem fairly easy. Just remember you have to walk all the way back up, too. Check with rangers about trail conditions, and check out our hiking tips (below). Trails can be found on both rims.

Trail Tips

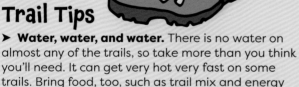

➤ **Water, water, and water.** There is no water on almost any of the trails, so take more than you think you'll need. It can get very hot very fast on some trails. Bring food, too, such as trail mix and energy bars.

➤ **See the bottom of the canyon?** You won't make it there and back in a day. Don't try!

➤ **Check the weather!** Even in summer, thunderstorms can come up suddenly; don't be caught with the wrong gear.

Hiking for the Family

Hiking together is one of the most fun things to do at the Grand Canyon. While some of the trails are very steep or long or difficult, there are plenty of places that even young hikers can enjoy with their family. Here are a few suggestions (but the same trail tips apply: bring lots of water and watch the weather!)

Bright Angel Trail Not too long, with a famous viewing point at the end. Leaves from near the Visitor Center on the South Rim. (There's also a Bright Angel Point on the North Rim.)

Rim Trail Which rim? The South! Families love this flat, partly paved trail that leads along the South Rim. It has lots of places to stop and ooh and ahh at the canyon view, plus gives a good look at South Rim forest life.

Roosevelt Point This is a very short trail on the North Rim. It combines a stroll through beautiful woods toward a great view of the canyon.

Cape Royal Trail On the North Rim and wheelchair accessible. Leads to a view of an incredible rock formation as well as the distant South Rim.

Bridle Trail On the North Rim, it's three miles long, but mostly flat and forested. A great way to experience life on the rims along with canyon views.

Grand Canyon National Park

Mule Rides

Why walk when you can ride? No, not cars or bikes—mules! Mules have long been a part of the Grand Canyon experience. You can take a day trip from the South Rim or North Rim. Don't worry, the mules know the trails! There are also overnight trips to the bottom of the canyon.

Early visitors used them as pack animals. The miners who worked the canyon depended on them, too. Since the National Park opened, mules have become a great way to safely travel into the canyon—and back up to the top!

Pro Tips!

➤ Mule riders have to be at least nine years old; sorry if you're not there yet!
➤ You have to speak English; believe it or not, the mules do!
➤ There are weight limits, too, so check with the mule-ride companies.

WARNING! If you're afraid of heights, mule rides are not for you! You'll be perched several feet above the trail. Some of the trails are on ledges that plunge into the canyon. If you're nervous about heights or riding, try another activity. The mules are very safe, but the experience can make some people (okay . . . me!) too nervous to enjoy it!

River Raft Trips

The first American explorers to reach the Grand Canyon did so on the Colorado River. Re-creating that journey is a wet-and-wild way to visit America's most famous hole in the ground. The park limits the number of people who can go on these trips, held from April to November, so plan ahead.

River Rafts These are large inflatable boats. Riders sit on top of the inflated sides; gear is stored in cases that form the seats. The flexible craft glide, wallow, bend, and curve as they twist and turn through rapids. Expert boat captains know every bend of the river. There are two ways these boats move down the river:

➤ **Two oars:** The expert captain does all the rowing and steering; riders just hang on!

➤ **Paddles:** Riders each help paddle the boat as it moves along.

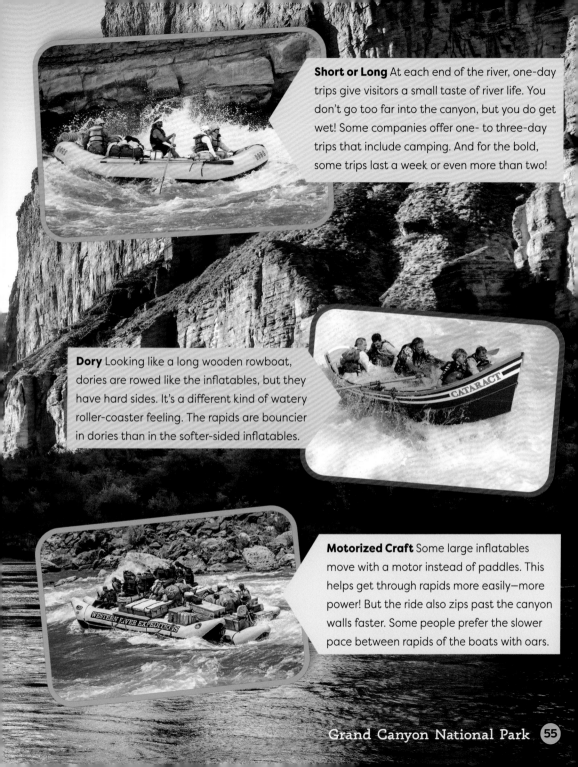

Short or Long At each end of the river, one-day trips give visitors a small taste of river life. You don't go too far into the canyon, but you do get wet! Some companies offer one- to three-day trips that include camping. And for the bold, some trips last a week or even more than two!

Dory Looking like a long wooden rowboat, dories are rowed like the inflatables, but they have hard sides. It's a different kind of watery roller-coaster feeling. The rapids are bouncier in dories than in the softer-sided inflatables.

Motorized Craft Some large inflatables move with a motor instead of paddles. This helps get through rapids more easily—more power! But the ride also zips past the canyon walls faster. Some people prefer the slower pace between rapids of the boats with oars.

On the River

You'll see millions of pictures of the Grand Canyon from above (plus dozens more in this book!). But what about the view from below! River rafters get to see that view as they cruise, bounce, spin, and bobble down the Colorado and its rapids from east to west.

Beaches: That's right . . . beaches! But no umbrellas or surfers here. Canyon beaches are great for pulling out rafts and setting up campsites. River guides know all the places, even as the river shifts the sand from year to year.

Amazing Rock Formations: Wind and water have carved the stone walls of the canyon into thousands of amazing shapes, some of which you can only see from the river.

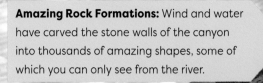

Waterfalls: Whether you see them from the river or on a hike during a stop, these towers of falling water against the brown cliffs make for a spectacular sight.

Caverns: The river not only carved the Grand Canyon, it carved side canyons rafters can see as they move along. Many trips also stop at huge cutouts like the Redwall Cavern.

Grand Canyon by Bike

Don't want to get wet? No problem! You can stay on the South Rim and explore amazing views from the comfort of your bike seat!

Hermit Road: On the South Rim, the Hermit Road, which goes west from the Bright Angel trailhead, is closed to cars during the summer (only park shuttle buses are allowed). But it's open to bikes!

South Rim Tours: Bright Angel Bikes offers tours and rental bikes for young and old alike. The tours go along South Rim bike trails, stopping often for great views.

North Rim Rides: Several trails on this rim are open to bikes, but there is not a place to rent . . . so bring your own!

Mountain Biking: Expert riders with the right gear can take on the Rainbow Rim single-track. It's 18 miles long, but you can do shorter parts of it. See the Kaibab Forest, canyon views, and maybe spot some local animals as you spin along. However, it's a long drive to reach the trail, so it's not for everyone. On the South Rim, tackle the 24-mile Arizona Trail.

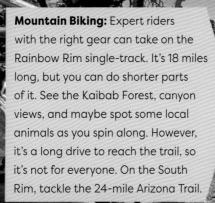

Animals and Plants

The big attraction at the Grand Canyon is, well, the canyon, of course. It might seem like the wildlife you see most walks on two feet and carries cameras, but Grand Canyon National Park is packed with real wildlife. It's also home to an amazing variety of trees, plants, and wildflowers. Put on your naturalist's hat and let's meet the locals!

Don't Feed the Squirrels!

Believe it or not, the animal that causes the most harm to humans in the canyon is this cute little guy. Bold and hungry squirrels have been coaxing treats from tourists for years. Sometimes, they bite fingers as well as food. Please don't feed them, as much as they seem to be begging you to!

Phabulous Photos

Try these tips for getting good wild animal photos on a phone camera:

➤ **Zoom.** Use your camera lens—not your feet!—to get closer.

➤ **Be Quiet.** Be as still and quiet as possible so you don't scare animals. Make sure your phone is on silent mode, too—they can hear that little "click."

➤ **Be Patient.** Don't try to coax animals into doing something. Wait until they're ready and you'll end up with better pictures.

➤ **Overdo It**. Use "burst" mode to get several shots in just a few seconds. You can go back later and pick out the best ones.

Who Lives Here?

Scientists and rangers have counted this many species living in the Grand Canyon National Park and nearby Kaibab National Forest.

Mammals: 91
Fish: 48
Reptiles: 17
Birds: 440

Mammals

Large and small mammals live in Grand Canyon National Park. Most of them find homes in the forests and plains along the rims of the canyon. The canyon is home to several large cats, as well as extremely cute and somewhat pesky squirrels and chipmunks.

Bobcat

Mule deer

Watch for Bison!

A herd of bison live in the forest on the north side of the canyon. Watch for them as you drive south on Highway 67 into the park.

Elk

Chipmunk

Kaibab squirrel

Bighorn sheep

Birds

The forests along the rim of the canyon are home to most of the bird species. They find homes in the trees and plenty to eat among the branches. The hot air that floats up from the canyon itself also means it is perfect flight space for raptors, who hover in the updraft while peering down for prey. Raptors of all kinds can be seen in the park, while others live near the river, hunting fish and insects that depend on the water.

Mexican spotted owl

California condor riding the hot air rising from the canyon.

Canyon raven

Canyon wren

Yellow-billed cuckoo

California Condor

This is the largest bird in North America, and one of the rarest. They almost went extinct, but breeding programs help the species survive. Now more than 400 live in and around the Grand Canyon. They are an incredible sight, with their 10-foot wingspan and their bright-pink heads sticking out of huge bodies.

Other Kinds of Animals

The hot, dry weather around much of the canyon is perfect for cold-blooded reptiles. Spiders and scorpions find prey and safety in the rocks and crevices. Down in the Colorado River, dozens of species of fish can be found.

Gila monster

Rattlesnake

Desert spiny lizard

Mojave desert tortoise

Humpback chub

Arizona bark scorpion

Grand Canyon Ecosystems

Looking at the Grand Canyon, you might think that it's all rocks and dirt. But there are five types of ecosystems in the park. An ecosystem is a small area of plants and animals who need similar conditions to thrive, including temperature, land, habitat, water, and more.

In all of the Grand Canyon's ecosystems, different plants thrive. In fact, there are more different species of plants in Grand Canyon National Park than in any other national park.

A big reason is the huge size and depth of the canyon, which creates many different microclimates and types of terrain. The canyon is unusual in having five different ecosystems, all in the same region.

Desert Scrub: Found at the canyon's lower elevations, it's a harsh, hot, and dry area in which only the toughest plants grow. You'll see yucca and cacti here, along with sagebrush. The park's reptiles mostly live in this area.

Mixed Conifer Forest: The North Rim gets the most rain and snow in the whole park. It is home to evergreens as well as deciduous (say "dih-SID-you-us") trees (that lose their leaves in winter). Because of the thick forest, it's home to lots of small mammals and birds.

Pinyon Juniper Forest: Below both rims, juniper and pinyon trees live alongside prickly pear cactus in areas that don't get much rain.

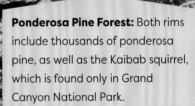

Ponderosa Pine Forest: Both rims include thousands of ponderosa pine, as well as the Kaibab squirrel, which is found only in Grand Canyon National Park.

Riparian: That's a fancy word for "near a river." The Colorado River banks are full of life, both plant and animal. The cottonwood tree can be seen above reed beds and river grasses. Mammals, insects, birds, and amphibians live along the banks, while fish live in the river.

Wildflowers
Everywhere!

One of the highlights of spring in the Grand Canyon is the growth of amazing wildflowers. This page shows just a few of them, which spring up after the winter snows thaw out and spring rains pour down.

Blue flax

Monkeyflower

Globemallow

Claret cup

Mojave aster

Grassleaf pea

Western
Redbud

What People Do in the Grand Canyon

Not everyone in Grand Canyon National Park is just visiting. Hundreds of people work on both rims. More work in the summer, of course, when they are there to greet thousands of tourists. Here's how they keep busy!

Park Rangers: The National Park Service has 50 full-time park rangers stationed at the Grand Canyon. They are in charge of protecting the park and its resources, while also educating and helping visitors. Along with being experts on the park and its natural resources, they are the first responders in case of emergency. What an important job to have!

River Raft Guides: Experts only! It takes years to become skilled enough to steer a raft or a dory full of tourists down the wet-and-wild Colorado River. Dozens work all summer long, making sure everyone makes it back safely—and wet.

Hiking and Mule-Trip Guides: Love the outdoors? Love helping people? Like mules? This might be a job for you someday. Guided hikes and mule trips are some of the most popular activities at the park. Guides not only keep visitors safe, they entertain and teach!

Train Workers: Choo-Choo! All aboard! The Grand Canyon Railway needs lots of folks to keep the trains on time. Engineers drive the train, conductors help passengers, and of course singing cowboys sing. Lots of other people work in the dining cars and at the stations at each end.

Restaurant/Hotel Workers: The number of servers, chefs, hotel workers, and cleaners skyrockets in the summer months. Hundreds of people are needed to make sure the canyon's many restaurants and hotels are all taken care of. Best part: A great view from your place of work!

Eating in the Grand Canyon

Birds, squirrels, lizards, and fish find their own food in Grand Canyon National Park. The human visitors need some help, though. Here are some places where you can grab some grub while you gaze in wonder at the marvelous Grand Canyon.

Bright Angel Café: Perfect for picknickers, this South Rim spot is the best place to grab a sandwich and some snacks before you settle into a viewing spot to marvel at the canyon itself. Bonus: You can rent bikes here once you're fully fueled up!

Phantom Ranch Canteen: The only way to enjoy the tasty food here is to hike *alllll* the way down to the bottom of the canyon. You'll need reservations way ahead of time. But if you make it down . . . and in . . . you'll enjoy home-cooked pancakes or tasty stews. *NOTE: Check ahead; repairs here might close the canteen for a while.*

Desert View Trading Post: Located to the east of Grand Canyon Village on the South Rim, this is the spot for ice cream—just right on a hot summer day!

El Tovar Dining Room: If mom and dad are feeling fancy, take them to this famous place. Take in spectacular views from the dining room while you dig into some of the best food for miles.

Canyon Village Market Place and Deli: It's not a supermarket, but it's in a super location. This South Rim store has everything your family will need to make up great meals, whether you're camping or staying in one of the hotels.

Yavapai Tavern: Love burgers? You'll love this place. It's on the South Rim in Grand Canyon Village. It's a great place to dig into a tasty burger after a day of hikes you'll never forget!

PLACES TO STAY

The most important part of finding a place to stay in the Grand Canyon is to plan ahead. It's one of the most popular national parks in the world, and there are many more visitors than places to sleep! Some people plan more than a year in advance! If your family can't get into one of these hotels or lodges, you could try camping (page 76) or staying at one of the many hotels outside the park to the north or south.

Bright Angel Lodge: This was the first official place to stay in the park. The original buildings opened in 1896. They've been modernized since then, but there's still a ton of history to see and explore. And the setting right on the South Rim is stunning!

El Tovar Hotel: Want to go fancy? Go here! This historic hotel was opened in 1905. Imagine what some of the first visitors to the national park experienced when you set foot in the huge lobby. The wood beams up ahead have seen some famous guests, too, including Pres. Theodore Roosevelt and famous scientist Albert Einstein.

Kachina Lodge/Thunderbird Lodge: These twin lodges are more modern, built in the 1960s. Both are right on the South Rim, so you'll get the views if not the history.

Maswik Lodge: The two buildings that make up this 1940s-era lodge are a bit farther from the canyon rim, but still just a short walk away.

Grand Canyon Lodge: This is the only indoor place to stay on the North Rim. It was built in 1937, after the original 1928 lodge burned down. Along with being a comfy place to rest, it has incredible views outside, plus cool historic design inside.

CAMPiNG!

Who needs roofs and showers and doors? Go camping! If you come to the Grand Canyon any time except winter, the weather is great for camping. Like the hotels, though, you have to plan ahead. There are a limited number of campsites and LOTS of people want them.

North Rim

FAST FACT
How to pack: It's easy to forget the bug spray, or the can opener, or the toilet paper. Check online for lists of stuff you'll definitely want to have with you.

North Rim Campground: There are only 90 spots in this small area, but it's right near the rim, so great views are easy to find.

South Rim

Mather Campground: This is the biggest one in the canyon, with 300 or more sites. You can't bring your family's RV here, but you can bring your car or your van and park near your site. A bonus is that this is open year-round!

Desert View Campground: Located about 25 miles east of the main Grand Canyon Village, this smaller site fills up fast, too. But if you can get in, it's great for groups of up to six people.

Trailer Village: If you're in a big RV, cruising around and seeing the country, this is the place to park it during your Grand Canyon visit—with a reservation, of course! Trailer Village has the hookups RVs need.

Bright Angel Campground/ Indian Garden Campground: Both of these are located below the South Rim. You'll have to hike (or take a mule) and carry all your gear with you.

Fossils in the Canyon

As the Colorado River carved away rocks and dirt to form the Grand Canyon, it revealed the canyon's past. For hundreds of millions of years, the Colorado Plateau had built up layer by layer. As each layer was formed, different animal and plant life was trapped. Since people began exploring the Grand Canyon, they have found signs of those animals–signs that have become fossils! There are three main kinds of fossils found in the Grand Canyon . . . and one kind that is not!

Land Animals Large and small mammals, small reptiles, and other land creatures left behind their marks. Explorers have found sloth skulls, reptile bones, and lots of tracks from smaller mammals preserved in the rocks in the canyon.

Where Are the Dinosaurs?

Everyone's favorite kind of fossil is from a dinosaur. So why are there no dinosaur fossils in the Grand Canyon? The answer is easy: All the dinosaurs were extinct (had died out) by the time the canyon really began being formed, only about 5-6 million yeras ago.

Worm tracks

Trilobites

Horn Coral

Ocean Animals At different points in the distant past, the canyon was under huge amounts of water. Animals that live in saltwater are called marine animals, and many left behind fossils to find. It's like a giant seashell hunt in the rocks of the canyon!

Plant Fossils Plants leave behind . . . leaves! Fossils also reveal stems and branches of long-dead ferns and similar plants.

Look, don't take! It's against the law to take any fossils away from the Grand Canyon.

STOP

Fossil Walks Park rangers lead fossil walks that show visitors evidence of animals and plants of the past. People can see fossils right in the rock. Fossils form when animals or plants die and their bodies slowly turn to rock over thousands of years. The rangers explain what the fossils reveal about the past and how old the fossils are.

Spooky Sights

Even when the night is quiet and the animals are asleep, you might not be alone in the Grand Canyon! Here are some spots some people think are haunted!

El Tovar Hotel: Is this the most haunted place in the Grand Canyon? Visitors have seen spirit forms "walking" down staircases. One family was welcomed to the hotel by a hotel worker—who then disappeared! And the hotel has the gravesite of Pirl Ward, who some think was a hotel worker long ago. Some people have seen Pirl's spooky form in a dark cloak on the hotel grounds.

Phantom Ranch: Well, *phantom* (which means "ghost") is right there in the name. So have ghosts really been seen down at this canyon-bottom camping and lodging spot? On the trail down to the ranch, visitors have seen a spirit form floating near the gravesite of Rees Griffith, a worker who was killed while building the trail. But the name of the ranch probably comes from the name of a nearby creek; the "phantom" part came from the fact that it had disappeared from an earlier map!

REES B. GRIFFITHS
TRAIL FOREMAN NATIONAL PARK SERVICE
BORN OCT. 26, 1873. DIED FEB. 6, 1922 IN
THE GRAND CANYON HE LOVED SO WELL AS
A RESULT OF INJURIES RECEIVED NEAR THIS
SPOT WHILE IN THE PERFORMANCE OF HIS
DUTY IN THE BUILDING OF THE
KAIBAB TRAIL

Ghosts in the Caverns: Located about a two-hour drive southwest of the main part of Grand Canyon National Park, the Grand Canyon Caverns have become a fun tourist stop. Guests take an elevator more than 200 feet down into huge, open, dry caverns for tours. But some of those guests report seeing the ghost of Walter Peck, one of the men who first found the caverns in the 1920s!

North Rim Wandering Woman: Wearing white and blue, this spooky form haunts the North Rim. The legends say that she jumped off the cliffs after her husband and son were killed in an accident. Camp workers and tourists say they have seen her— or have they? Keep an eye out at sunset; that's when she often appears.

Canyon Stargazing

When's the best time to see tons of stars? In the dark sky at night, of course. And since there is very little light from human sources in and around the Grand Canyon, the stargazing here is awesome! In fact, the entire park is officially a Dark Sky Park. That means that not only does nature provide great darkness, but that the park buildings and lighting at night are designed to make it easier for visitors to see stars.

Legends in the Sky: The stars and the night sky are part of legends and stories told by Native Americans who live near the park. The Navajo say that the First Woman made the sun from quartz, and then sprinkled the leftover rocks into the sky as the stars. Carvings made by the ancient Anasazi show that they tracked the movement of stars and might have witnessed a supernova more than 1,200 years ago.

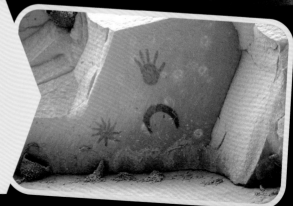

What's Up There?: Even without a telescope, at the right times of year you can see up to six planets in the sky over the Grand Canyon. On cloudless nights, see the amazing Milky Way (Earth's home galaxy!). Look for constellations including Orion, stars like Polaris, and maybe even watch the International Space Station drift by.

Stargazing Tips

➤ You'll need a flashlight, of course, so you don't trip while walking to a good viewing spot. But use a red lens on your light. This will help you have better night vision.

➤ Once you're in your spot, wait about 20 or 30 minutes without any light. This will help you see even more stars as your eyes adjust to the darkness.

➤ Temperatures can drop quickly at night; bring extra clothes or blankets to stay warm, even in spring and summer.

Star Parties: We're not talking movie stars here, but millions of twinkling lights in the sky. In June, come for the Grand Canyon Star Party. Use powerful telescopes to see even farther into space. The Flagstaff Star Party is in the fall, with experts from the nearby Lowell Observatory.

Not Far Away

As if the Grand Canyon was not enough, other nearby sites offer ways to explore the natural beauty and history of the area.

We went to another hole in the ground!

What? The Grand Canyon wasn't enough?

Well, yes, it was awesome, but so was this!

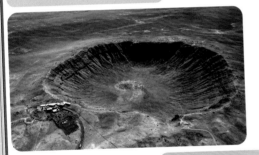

😮 That is HUGE!

It's **Meteor Crater**! It was made 50,000 years ago by a huge meteor.

Glad we weren't there to watch!

Very cool. Astronauts trained there before going to the moon!

It's about 40 miles east of Flagstaff.

Hope you didn't drive into it!

Ha! It's hard to miss! There's also a museum at the edge.

Any cool stuff?

Yes! Lots of amazing rocks and minerals and space stuff!

Nice. Hope we don't get hit with another meteor!

We took another time-traveling trip.

Not another meteor, I hope.

Nope, this was a bit more recent—only about 1,100 years ago.

That's not exactly recent!

We visited **Wupatki**, near Flagstaff.

Looks like it needs some work.

It's old, dude! These are ruins of a building used by Ancestral Puebloans.

Oh, good. I thought it was a gift shop! 😀

Uh . . . no. These are some of the biggest ruins left in the area.

The word means "tall house" in the Hopi language.

Not exactly a skyscraper, huh?

Well, they didn't have cranes back then! They say about 100 people might have lived here.

Nice! Where did they go?

Experts say the people all left around 1225. But no one knows where they went!

Look! Up in the sky!

What? Where?

No . . . just look! That's what we did here.

It's the **Lowell Observatory**. It was named for Percival Lowell, who built it in 1894.

That's one mighty big telescope!

Actually, it's a pretty small one, but it has a big history.

Lowell looked for Planet X, which he thought was beyond Neptune.

Did he find it?

No, but in 1929, another astronomer did.

Who?

Clyde Tombaugh found Lowell's Planet X. He called it Pluto!

Wait, Pluto's not a planet!

Well, it was called one for a long time. Now it's a dwarf planet, but it was first seen from right here in Arizona!

On our way back home, we made an awesome stop.

For gas and snacks?

Well, of course, but I'm talking about this place.

Did they fill the Grand Canyon with water?

Ha! No, this is **Lake Mead**. It's on the Colorado River, too. It was created in 1935 when they put up a huge dam.

You can't say dam.

Not even my dad would make a joke that bad.

It's about a 3-4 hour drive from Grand Canyon Village. Thousands of people visit each year to boat and swim and fish.

Splish, splash!

You can bike, hike, kayak, or even ride horses!

No horses for me, thanks!

No problem. Lake Mead has less water than in the past. The West is going through a big drought.

Glad you stopped for snacks and water!

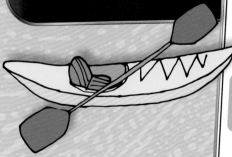

Other Amazing Parks

There are more than 420 National Parks in the United States; Grand Canyon is by far the deepest! But not far from the Grand Canyon are several other amazing national parks that are worth a visit. (And who knows: maybe they'll be a new book in SUPER PARKS! someday, too!)

Bryce Canyon National Park: There are more hoodoos here than anywhere else on Earth. What's a hoodoo? That's the name for the tall, bumpy, rock formations shown here. Formed over millions of years by water eroding rock, the sandstone towers are a highlight of this Utah park. Walk or ride horses among the towers of this unique landscape.

Zion National Park: Want to walk in a river? Head to this National Park, also in Utah. While the Colorado River carved the Grand Canyon, here the Virgin River carved a different sort of "hole" called a slot canyon. At the right time of year, visitors can walk into these tall but very narrow canyons for an otherworldly (if slightly damp) adventure.

Arches and Canyonlands National Parks:
Take one guess where Arches National Park got its name! Erosion created a landscape of amazing arches, rock formations, and towering bluffs. In both parks, hike or drive through these formations. Keep your camera ready for amazing sunset and sunrise images in the Utah desert.

Death Valley National Park: The hottest place in the United States is usually at the bottom of this sandy valley in California. Some areas are almost 300 feet (91 m) below sea level, the lowest place in the US. But spring and fall are lovely here in the desert.

Petrified Forest National Park: East of the Grand Canyon in Arizona is this one-of-a-kind place. Over thousands of years, the hot, dry climate turned trees into stone, mostly quartz—they became petrified. As the land moved, the giant stone trees cracked, and their remains are scattered over the landscape, perfect for you to explore on your visit there.

Websites, Books, and More!

Web Sites

National Park Service, Grand Canyon
https://www.nps.gov/grca

National Park Service Grand Canyon Site for Kids
https://www.nps.gov/grca/learn/kidsyouth/index.htm

National Geographic Kids
https://kids.nationalgeographic.com/nature/article/
grand-canyon

Native Americans and the Grand Canyon
https://www.mygrandcanyonpark.com/park/
native-americans/native-american-tribes/

Outside Magazine Tips for Kids
https://www.mygrandcanyonpark.com/things-to-do/
park-itineraries/kids-activities-grand-canyon/

Books

Chin, Jason. *Grand Canyon.* Roaring Brook, 2017.

Lomberg, Michelle. *Grand Canyon.* Weigl, 2019.

London, Martha. *Grand Canyon (Engineered by Nature).* Kids Core, 2022.

Mahoney, Emily. *20 Fun Facts About the Grand Canyon.* Gareth Stephens, 2019.

O'Connor, Jim. *Where Is the Grand Canyon?* Penguin Workshop, 2015.

Parker, Katie. *Grand Canyon National Park (Field Guide).* Pebble, 2020.

Photo Credits and Thanks

Photos are primarily from the National Park Service's extensive media and historical collection; most of the contemporary images are by Michael Quinn/NPS. Other photos come from Dreamstime, Library of Congress, National Archives, Shutterstock, or Wikimedia.

Artwork: Lemonade Pixel; Maps (6-7) by Jessica Nevins. Cover typography by Swell Type.

Thanks to our pals Nancy Ellwood, Kait Leggett, and the fine folks at Arcadia!

INDEX

Thanks for Visiting

GRAND CANYON NATIONAL PARK

Come Back Soon!